east
west
STYLE

ROCKPORT

east
west
STYLE

**A Design Guide for
Blending Eastern and Western
Elements at Home**

Ann McArdle

GLOUCESTER MASSACHUSETTS

ROCKPORT PUBLISHERS

First published in the United States of America by
Rockport Publishers, Inc.
33 Commercial Street
Gloucester, Massachusetts 01930-5089
Telephone: (978) 282-9590
Facsimile: (978) 283-2742
www.rockpub.com

ISBN 1-56496-655-0

10 9 8 7 6 5 4 3

Design: Kristen Webster
Layout: SYP Design & Production
Front Cover Photo: Matteo Manduzio
    courtesy of Zimmer & Rohde
    Zimmersmuhlenweg 14-18
    D-61440 Oberursel
    Telephone: 06171-632-146
    Fax: 06171-632-244
Back Cover Photos:
    Top: Photo: Jacques Dirand
            Design: Christian Liaigre
    Center: Photo: Clark Quinn
            Design: Peter Forbes and Associates
    Bottom: Design: Roche Bobois
Contents page image:
        Photo: Paul Ferrino
        Design: Peter Forbes

Printed in China.

Photo: www.davidduncanlivingston.com

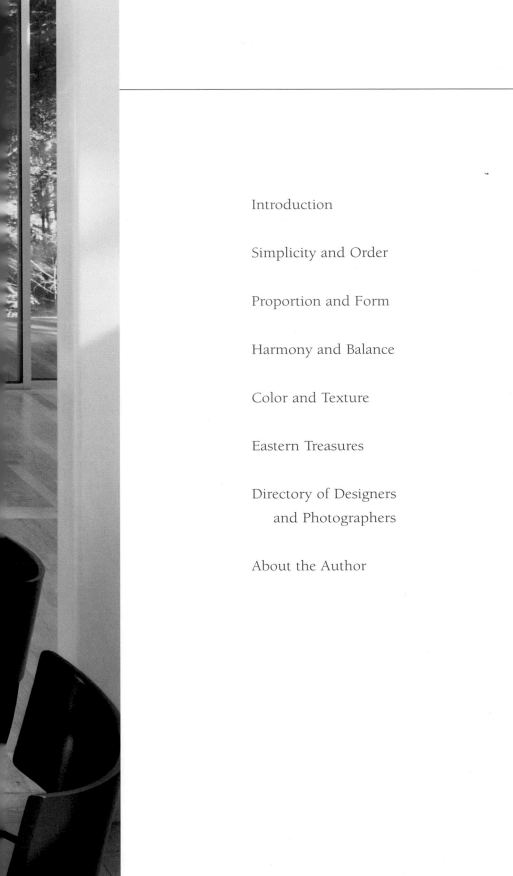

contents

introduction

THINK OF THE EAST AND WHAT COMES TO MIND? A CONTEM-
PLATIVE JAPANESE GARDEN? A SHINTO TEMPLE? A CHINESE
PAGODA? CHERRY BLOSSOMS? The serenity that lies beneath these
images is the core of the Eastern element of East-West style.
Incorporated into Western traditions of grand scale and elaborate
decoration, the result is a toned down, restful ambience representing
the blend of sensibilities from diverse cultures with universal appeal.

To Westerners, once enigmatic Far Eastern traditions have
become increasingly familiar. Technological innovations in this century
have improved not just the way we travel and exchange information,
but how we think about the world. We are more aware of the concerns
of all nations in real time. This facilitation of international experience
has led naturally to fuller cultural awareness among people of the
world.

Now, through travel or the media, we are at least conversant
with the images of far away places. Ethnic restaurants provide
opportunities to experience the ambience of different cultures.
International trade has given us easy access to goods originating in
distant lands. Familiarity leads to appreciation and appreciation leads to
imitation. One culture assimilates the best of another, resulting in a new
look comprised of the best of the best.

Photo: www.davidduncanlivingston.com / Design: Carol Shawn Interiors

Photo: Courtesy of Lightolier

At the same time that technology increases our awareness of other cultures, the rapid rate of travel and information transfer has drastically intensified our lives. The expectation of instant results has led to a frenetic daily pace for many of us. Simplicity, a key component in much Eastern design, has therefore become especially appealing. Westerners are moving away from the idea of home as showpiece and entertainment space to home as a place for repose and calm, balancing the hectic pace of daily life with a serene refuge.

Photo: Steve Vierra / Design: Growing Spaces

Incorporate the Asian elements of harmony, simplicity, and proportion into your decór for an invitingly tranquil home. Balance light and dark, rough and smooth, linear and curvilinear. Use a minimum of decorative accessories, clean window treatments, and unfussy furnishings. Pay attention to relative size and shapes of furnishings as well as the overall form of the space. Use bold color to enliven a room or earthy tones to quiet a busy corner. Use a variety of textures to spark a monochromatic interior. Add an exotic touch with a carefully positioned Eastern treasure.

In *East-West Style* we present examples of these elements in a variety of interiors to inspire your own application of them. While the features are not exclusive of each other, each one is essential to the whole. Simplicity and order is dependent upon harmony and balance, which is dependent upon geometric proportion and form. Suitable use of color and texture supports all of these essential components and without it the others lack spirit. Varying the emphasis produces a broad range of distinctive looks. Blend the aesthetics of the Far East with those of the West to transform your home into one that embodies the best of both worlds as it reflects your personal style.

simplicity and
order

SIMPLICITY IS ESSENTIAL TO JAPANESE DESIGN AND A DOMINANT FEATURE IN EAST-WEST INTERIORS. According to Eastern religions and philosophies, such as Buddhism, Taoism, and Shintoism, simplicity is a way of life. From this tradition, the principles of Japanese design evolved—moderation, restraint in the use of materials and space, and unpretentiousness.

Toning down visual stimuli can create a restful ambience. A sparely furnished room in a quiet color scheme with carefully placed accents can be as lovely as a fully appointed palace. Take the Japanese garden, for example. Components are laid out in specific patterns to promote contemplation. Scale and placement are of utmost importance, as is impeccable maintenance. These design elements can be imitated in Western interiors for similar effect.

MAKE AN ELEGANT STATEMENT WITH THE BAREST ELEMENTS. HERE A VANITY SINK WITH MINIMALIST FIXTURES RESTS ON A STONE SLAB TO CREATE AN EXOTIC BATH WITH A PURE SPIRIT.

Photo: David Story

Interior Designer: George Suyama

Lighting Designer: Christopher Thompson

feng shui
basics

FROM CHINA THE ART OF PLACEMENT, *FENG SHUI*, ASSESSES
LOCATIONS FOR THE OPTIMAL ACCOMMODATION OF *CH'I*,
ENERGY. One of *Feng Shui's* main tenets is the reduction of clutter:
too many objects stifle energy, causing the inhabitants to become
lethargic or uninspired. Even without espousing the ancient Chinese
beliefs, one can see the truth in this. At one time or another everyone
has experienced a sense of defeat when faced with a messy office or
an overstuffed closet, and the release that follows the straightening up
or weeding out of the cluttered space.

Photo: Tim Hursley / Architecture: Peter Forbes

Photo: Clark Quinn / Architecture and Table Design: Peter Forbes and Associates

(opposite) CHOOSE A LONG DINING TABLE WITH SQUARE, CLEAN LEGS FOR A SPARE, SIMPLE
LOOK. BRING OUT CHAIRS ONLY WHEN NEEDED TO ADD DRAMA. A LONE BOWL OF GREEN
APPLES OFF-CENTER ON THE TABLE COMPLETES THIS MINIMALIST STATEMENT.

(above) IN AN OPEN FLOOR PLAN, CONCEAL THE CLUTTER OF FOOD PREPARATION. A SIMPLE
EDGE AROUND THE KITCHEN ISLAND SHIELDS DIRTY POTS AND PANS FROM VIEW WHILE
DINERS ENJOY A RELAXING MEAL. A WALL OF FLAT FRONT CABINETS FORMS A CLEAN
BACKDROP AND PROVIDES PLENTY OF STORAGE SPACE.

Photo: Matthew Millman / Design: Fu Tung Cheng

A simple floor plan and an orderly room gives one freedom from this sense of weight and sets the stage for an East-West look. If clutter is a problem for you, chests with drawers can serve as end tables, providing a place to stash odds and ends out of sight. Use accessories sparingly just to enliven otherwise dead space or to introduce color where needed. Each piece is given importance by light, space, and position: Accent individual elements with lighting to enhance their presence. Consider the space around an object as an element in its own right. Just as in a symphony the silent moments are part of the music, in a room the space around an object is part of the décor. Given enough breathing room, an accent can become more effective.

(opposite) ENJOY THE CONVENIENCE OF CASUAL MEALS
IN THE KITCHEN WITH A DINING NOOK IN AN AIRY
WINDOW BAY. INSTALL MINIMALIST FURNISHINGS WITH
SLEEK SURFACES FOR A SERENE OASIS IN THE HEART
OF THE ACTION.

(right) DESIGN A PEACEFUL ARRANGEMENT IN THE
ENTRYWAY TO SET THE MOOD OF YOUR HOME. THE
WARM HONEY OAK OF THIS UNASSUMING CHEST
PICKS UP THE COLOR IN THE AUTUMN LANDSCAPE
PAINTING ABOVE AND PROVIDES A STRAIGHTFORWARD
BASE FOR AN UNDERSTATED DISPLAY SYMBOLIC OF
NATURE'S BOUNTY.

Photo: Steve Vierra / Interior Design: Marian Glasgow

Use a lacquered Chinese chest or Japanese *tansu* as an element of interest that provides valuable storage space. Let decorative pieces double as storage in the bathroom. A guest towel stored in a Japanese incense burner is attractive and convenient. Let a sofa with clean lines provide seating. Extra pillows stacked in a corner can accommodate overflow. Choose *Shoji*-type screens to dress a window without introducing mass. Build your decor around a central piece of art, using its colors as your guide. Keep a coffee table free of clutter. A small plant or sculptural piece gives it life. Plenty of light contributes to a feeling of spaciousness. If you're short on natural light, flood your walls with artificial light. Place a single potted plant where it can be viewed from all sides. The graceful lines of orchids work especially well within the Eastern aesthetic. Hang a *tatami* on the wall above your bed for a headboard.

Photo: Matthew Millman / Interior Design: Orlando Diaz-Azcuy Designs

Photo: Art Gray / Interior Design: Hagy Belzberg

(opposite) KEEP THE BEDROOM FURNISHINGS SPARE AND USE A CHINESE SCREEN AT THE HEAD OF THE BED FOR INTEREST. PLAIN WALLS AND BEDDING PROVIDE A RESTFUL LOOK, BUT THE ADDITION OF SUBTLE TEXTURE IN THE COVERLET BALANCES THE IMPACT OF THE SCREEN.

(above) LET LEVEL CHANGES DELINATE SEPARATE AREAS IN AN OPEN FLOOR PLAN. FURNISH WITH SLEEK, LOW SEATING AND GLASS-TOPPED TABLES FOR A CLEAN LOOK. LINK FURNISHINGS TO ARCHITECTURAL ELEMENTS FOR UNITY. THE LEGS OF THIS COFFEE TABLE SUBTLY RESTATE THE FORM OF THE CHIMNEY.

Photo: Courtesy of Lightolier

(opposite) IN AN OPEN KITCHEN/DINING AREA, SHIELD THE CLUTTER OF FOOD PREPARATION WITH A SOLID ISLAND. THE MATERIALS AND LINES OF THIS KITCHEN'S SURFACES ILLUSTRATE THAT SIMPLE IS NOT SYNONYMOUS WITH BORING.

(above) CREATE A SERENE AMBIANCE BY ILLUMINATING EASTERN-STYLE FURNISHINGS WITH A SHOJI-LIKE FIXTURE.

Photo and Design: Charlotte Jensen

(above) IN A SMALL HOME DEFINE AREAS OF ACTIVITY WITH SHOJI SCREENS. DIFFUSE LIGHT THROUGH THE TRANSLUCENT SCREEN ALLOWS THE USE OF BOLD COLORS FOR ACCENT WALLS. CREATE AN EXOTIC WALL ORNAMENT WITH A SIMPLE SWAG OF ASIAN FABRIC DRAPED OVER A ROD.

(opposite) LET AN ORIENTAL SPA PROVIDE INSPIRATION FOR THE SIMPLE PLEASURES OF BATHING. SURROUND A LARGE STAINLESS STEEL TUB WITH EARTHY TEXTURES AND COLORS FOR A LUXURIOUS BLEND OF FORM AND FUNCTION.

MAKE YOUR BATHROOM A PEACEFUL GETAWAY WITH LINENS AND SUPPLIES HIDDEN BEHIND FLAT-FRONT CABINETS. UPLIGHTING CONCEALED ABOVE THE CABINETS BRIGHTENS THE ROOM AND RELAXES THE ATMOSPHERE.

(above) CHOOSE MINIMALIST FURNISHINGS TO GIVE A BEDROOM EAST-WEST APPEAL. THIS LOW PLATFORM BED

GETS ITS CHARM FROM THE UNDULATING LINE OF THE MATTRESS SURROUND. AN ARMOIRE WITH A MATTE LACQUER

FAÇADE CONCEALS CLOTHING AND ADDS A SHOJI-SCREEN LOOK TO ITS SLIDING DOORS. A SMATTERING OF NATURAL

ACCESSORIES GIVES THE ROOM LIFE.

(opposite) USE EASTERN ARTIFACTS TO KEEP SUPPLIES HANDY WITHOUT CLUTTERING AN ORDERLY BATHROOM. THE

ELEMENTS ENHANCE THE DÉCOR WHILE SERVING AS MORE THAN JUST ADORNMENT.

Photo: Jeff McNamara / Design: Austin Patterson Disston

(above) GIVE A TINY BATHROOM A SERENE APPEARANCE WITH A SOLID TUB
SURROUND IN A RESTFUL EARTHY TONE. THE FLAT SURFACE QUIETS THE EYE AND
DIMINISHES THE ENCLOSED FEELING OF THE TIGHT QUARTERS.

(opposite) CREATE A LOOK OF UNADORNED ELEGANCE IN THE BATHROOM WITH
POLISHED MARBLE SURFACES AND FLAT FRONT CABINETS. A SCULPTED ABOVE-THE-
COUNTER SINK SOFTENS THE LOOK WITH ITS CURVES.

(above) USE WOODEN OVERLAYS ON WINDOWS SUCH AS THESE TO PROVIDE PRIVACY WHILE ALLOWING LIGHT TO FILTER THROUGH. THE VERTICAL SLATS PROVIDE TEXTURAL INTEREST AND ENHANCE THE GRAIN OF THE FLOOR. THE UNADORNED BEAUTY OF THE SPACE IS BOTH RESTFUL AND ELEGANT.

(opposite top) MATCH WINDOW SHUTTERS TO WALL COLOR TO MAKE A ROOM'S BOUNDARIES RECEDE. SPARE FURNISHINGS WITH BOLD LINES IN COMPLEMENTARY WOODS AND NEUTRAL TONES INVITE REST AND RELAXATION.

(opposite bottom) INCORPORATE YOUR HEADBOARD INTO THE STRUCTURE OF THE BEDROOM ADDING ARCHITECTURAL INTEREST WITH A CLEAN, SLEEK LOOK. A MIRROR-LINED ALCOVE PROVIDES INTEREST WITHOUT ADDING MASS AND VISUALLY EXPANDS THE ROOM.

Photo: Poliform

Photo: Colin McRae / Design: Charles Stewart

Photo: Courtesy of Luminaire

(above) TIGHTLY TUCK A DAYBED'S COVER TO KEEP THE LOOK SPARE AND
RESTFUL. MONOCHROMATIC GEOMETRIC ACCENTS ADD INTEREST TO THIS ROOM
WITHOUT TAINTING ITS UNADORNED FEELING.

(opposite) PLACE A CONSOLE TABLE AT THE HEAD OF YOUR BED TO
ACCOMMODATE READING LAMPS WHILE KEEPING THE ROOM SPARE AND
UNCLUTTERED. CHOOSE FLAT PANELED CLOSET DOORS AND MINI BLINDS THE
COLOR OF THE WALLS FOR A PRISTINE BACKDROP. SEDATE WEDGE-WOOD BLUE
FOR CARPET AND COMFORTER ADDS COLOR INTEREST AND MAINTAINS THE
SERENE LOOK.

Design: Rick Mather Architects / Photo: Dennis Gilbert/Arcaid

Photo: Tim Street-Porter

(above) SURRENDER YOUR BEDROOM TO THE EASTERN AESTHETIC. LET A FUTON ON THE
FLOOR SERVE AS THE BED. HERE THE RICE PAPER LIGHT FIXTURE AND BED COVERING OF
LINEAR ABSTRACT DESIGN SEAL THE MOOD.

(opposite) A WESTERN DINING ROOM TAKES ON EASTERN SERENITY WITH UNADORNED
FURNISHINGS AND A NEUTRAL COLOR PALETTE. SURROUND A LIGHT WOOD TABLE WITH
UPHOLSTERED CHAIRS IN A NEUTRAL, TEXTURED FABRIC TO COMPLEMENT A NATURAL COIR
RUG UNDERFOOT. VELVET TO MATCH THE DARK BUFFET UNITES AND QUIETS THE SPACE.

Photo: Nick Wheeler / Design: Peter Forbes

proportion and
form

SCALE PLAYS AN OBVIOUS ROLE IN THE CHOICE OF FURNISHINGS FOR A HOME. A large room looks more comfortable with large-scale furniture. An overstuffed sofa with a high back and sweeping arms in a small room, however, can overpower the space and obstruct easy movement through the room. Beyond this obvious attention to proportion within a space, however, the Eastern aesthetic relies on the repetition of form balanced by the introduction of an opposing shape. The Japanese have mastered the use of geometric order and employ congruous, compatible, orderly lines to create a pleasing whole. In interior décor the same order can be applied, integrating the furnishings and the space as a whole.

CURVED INTERIOR WALLS SOFTEN A LARGE AREA ADDING GRACE TO A LONG CORRIDOR. A CONICAL COFFEE SERVICE PROVIDES WHIMSICAL RELIEF TO THE CLEAN LINES OF THE KITCHEN WHILE MAINTAINING THE SPARE THEME.

point–
counterpoint

SHOJI SCREENS OFFER A GRID OF STRAIGHT LINES INTERSECTING AT RIGHT ANGLES AS A REFERENCE FOR SHAPES AND PLACEMENT OF FURNISHINGS. Repeat the angles with straight lines in the furniture. The resulting ordered series of squares or rectangles, however, will need to be softened. Introduce an incongruous angle or curve with a striking accent piece. A leafy plant can act as counterpoint to a strictly angular décor. Or use the pattern of upholstery fabrics to ease the rigidity.

Examine the dimensions of the room. A room with vaulted ceilings needs focus at eye level to keep from feeling austere. Low, sloping ceilings require special treatment to open up the room. You can turn the room's limitations into advantages: Put low sleek furnishings under the eaves. An attention-getting piece at the roof ridge to bring attention to that area. Look at the silhouettes of furnishings, from all angles, to see the impact of their shapes. If the grouping is too homogeneous, add an element of surprise to relieve the monotony. If the forms are discordant, link them with like colors or patterns, or remove a piece or two. Sparse furnishings are better than wrong furnishings.

Photo: www.davidduncanlivingston.com

Photo: Roger Williams Hotel / Design: Unique Hotels and Resorts

(opposite) SET A SQUARE DINING TABLE AND BOXY CHAIRS IN FRONT OF LIGHT SHOJI-TYPE SCREENS FOR A STUDY IN STRAIGHT LINES, BOTH HORIZONTAL AND VERTICAL. RELAX THE ORDERED, GEOMETRIC LOOK WITH A PENDANT LIGHT FIXTURE THAT LOOKS LIKE A PIECE OF SILK FLOATING IN THE AIR.

(above) IN A SMALL ROOM, USE A SHOJI SCREEN TO CREATE A FLOOR-TO-CEILING VISUAL LINK BETWEEN TWO BEDS. MATCH THE WOOD AND FORM OF THE SCREEN WITH UNADORNED FOOT BOARDS. PUFFY PILLOWS AND DUVETS KEEP THE ROOM FROM APPEARING STARK.

Photo: John Martin / Lighting Design: Becca Foster / Interior Design: Michael Harris

(above) USE HALF-WALLS TO DEFINE A DINING SPACE WITHOUT DETRACTING FROM AN OPEN-
FLOOR PLAN. A HANGING ORIENTAL SCREEN ECHOES THE LINE OF THE PANELS IN THE
PARTITION AS VIEWED FROM THE LIVING AREA. USE NATURAL COLORS AND UNOBTRUSIVE
LIGHT FIXTURES FOR AN AIRY QUALITY.

(opposite) SCALE ACCESSORIES TO FOLLOW THE CURVE OF AN ARCHED STAIR WALL. A TALL
VASE OF SPIDERY BRANCHES AND FLOWERS PLACED AT THE HIGH END OF THE WALL ADDS
THE NECESSARY DIMENSION TO THE ENTRYWAY FURNISHINGS. CHOOSE A TABLE THAT ECHOES
THE STYLE OF THE ARCHITECTURE TO FURTHER UNIFY THE LOOK.

☛ Instead of blocking windows with a bulky headboard, tuck a low platform bed below the sills. ☛ Add height to ceilings with vertical lines and low furnishings. ☛ Play with lighting on intricate filigrees or plants to cast shadows heightening their impact. ☛ In a room with strong horizontals, use pendant lighting or tall artifacts to add a vertical element.

Photo: Alan Weintraub / Design: Fu Tung Cheng

Photo: Douglas Salin / Lighting Design: Linda Ferry / Interior Design: John Schneider / Architecture: William David Martin

(opposite) TAKE ADVANTAGE OF POST-AND-BEAM CONSTRUCTION TO FRAME
SEPARATE SPACES IN AN OPEN FLOOR PLAN. DEFINE A CENTRAL PATHWAY
WITH LIGHTING AND ARTWORK PLACED AT THE END WALL.

(above) BALANCE ANGULAR ARCHITECTURAL DETAILS WITH A ROUND DINING
TABLE AND INVITING WICKER ARMCHAIRS WITH CURVY LINES. TALL
CANDLESTICKS REACH FOR A SOARING CEILING AND SUBTLY LIMIT THE
HEIGHT OF THE DINING SPACE.

Photo: Steve Vierra / Design: Marcia Connors

(opposite) IN A CONTEMPORARY HOME WITH OPEN CEILINGS CREATE AN ELEGANT
EASTERN FEEL WITH A PRESENTATION OF ORCHIDS ON THE SIMPLEST OF TABLES,
TOPPED WITH A LARGE MIRROR TO REFLECT THE EFFECT AND OPEN THE SPACE. USE
LIGHTING TO ACCENT FLOWERS AND PLANTS, ADDING TO THE DRAMA.

(above) SOFTEN THE STRONG GEOMETRIC PRESENCE OF A SHOJI SCREEN WITH A
SLEEK SCULPTURAL STORK AND A VASE OF LONG WISPY BRANCHES OF A
BLOSSOMING CHERRY. EACH ELEMENT BEARS STRONG EASTERN SYMBOLISM WHILE
CREATING A LOVELY AND RESTFUL CORNER.

Photo: Douglas Salin
Lighting and Interior Design: Carla Carstens, ASID, CID
Architecture: Michael Helm

Photo: Russell Abraham / Design: Don Maxcy

(above) INCORPORATE A JAPANESE-STYLE TABLE INTO THE DINING AREA WITH A FLOOR TREATMENT TO CONTINUE THE LINE OF THE TABLE. THE EXTENDED LINE DEFINES THE AREA IN AN OPEN FLOOR PLAN AND SETS THE STAGE FOR EXOTIC ENTERTAINING IN THE EASTERN TRADITION.

(opposite) RETAIN THE SYMMETRY OF A FIREPLACE WALL BALANCED WITH LARGE WINDOWS ON EITHER SIDE. SITUATE TWO SOFAS FACING EACH OTHER ACROSS A SQUARE COFFEE TABLE IN FRONT OF THE FIREPLACE. HERE THE CLEAN HORIZONTAL LINES OF THE MANTEL AND RAISED HEARTH LINK THE TWO SIDES. COILED LIGHT FIXTURES SOFTEN THE STRAIGHT LINES.

Photo: John Sutton / Lighting Design and Architecture: Dan Phipps, AIA

Photo and Lighting Design: Alfredo Zaparolli / Interior Design: Rosemary Wilton

Photo: Luis Ferreira Alves / Architecture: Eduardo Souto Moura

(above) LET DELICATE LATTICEWORK CHAIRBACKS CREATE SHADOW PATTERNS ON THE FLOOR. ECHO THE PATTERN IN THE BASE OF A CHINESE PORCELAIN BOWL TO UNIFY THE SPACE.

(left) EVEN A DOOR CAN BECOME AN ARTISTIC STATEMENT AND PROVIDE ADORNMENT WITHOUT CLUTTER. HERE A SIMPLE GEOMETRIC CUTOUT PATTERN GIVES THE DOOR AND ITS SURROUNDINGS ADDED PRESENCE.

(opposite) USE STORAGE SPACE AS A MEANS FOR INTRODUCING AN EASTERN PATTERN. THE STRIKING GEOMETRIC DESIGN OF THIS MEDIA CENTER SETS THE THEME FOR THE ROOM. ITS LINES ARE REPEATED IN THE FURNISHINGS AND SOFTENED WITH THE WISPY POTTED TREE.

Photo: Warren Jagger / Interior Design: Techler Design Group

Photo: Eric Roth / Interior Design: Machine Age

(above) IN A LOFT USE SHOJI SCREENS TO PROVIDE DEFINITION, PRIVACY, AND A STRONG GEOMETRIC STATEMENT. SYMMETRICAL ARRANGEMENT OF ANGULAR SEATING ADDS TO THE EAST-WEST LOOK.

(opposite) IN A ROOM WHERE THE ARCHITECTURE PRESENTS A SERIES OF SURFACES CHOOSE RECTANGULAR, FLAT-BACKED SEATING FOR PLANE-ON-PLANE INTERPLAY. AN ANGULAR LAMP AND WISPY CAT O' NINE TAILS RELIEVE THE STRONG GEOMETRY AND DEFINE THE ROOM'S DEPTH. SMOOTH STONES ON THE HEARTH INTRODUCE THE EASTERN SYMBOLISM FOR WATER.

Photo: Dennis Gilbert/Arcaid / Design: Rick Mather

(opposite) OPEN UP AN ATTIC ROOM WITH NATURAL LIGHT FROM SKYLIGHTS. FLOOR CUSHIONS TRICK THE EYE AND PULL THE FOCUS DOWN. LOW, HORIZONTAL FURNISHINGS EMPHASIZE THE BREADTH OF THE ROOM.

(above) CHOOSE WINDOW TREATMENTS FOR THE LIGHT THEY ADMIT AS WELL AS THEIR APPEARANCE. VENETIAN MINI BLINDS CAST STRIPS OF LIGHT ARTICULATING THE STRONG LINES OF OPEN SHELVING AND HARDWOOD FLOORS. ANGULAR SEATING AND SPIKY PLANTS ADD ENERGY WHILE OFFSETTING THE ORDERED GEOMETRY.

(opposite) FOR AN ATTIC BEDROOM, A FLOOR FUTON SUITS THE SLANTED CEILINGS. ORNAMENTAL
GLOBES RELIEVE THE CONVERGING LINES OF THE WALL AND CEILING. PLACE A TALL SCULPTURAL PIECE
OR PLANTS IN THE AREA UNDER THE RIDGE TO DRAW ATTENTION TO THE OPEN SPACE. THE FRAMED
PRINTS OBSCURE THE EDGE OF THE EAVES GIVING THE ILLUSION OF ADDED HEIGHT.

Photo: Courtesy of the Morson Collection

(above) FIT A PLATFORM BED AGAINST A LOW WINDOW LEDGE LEAVING THE
WINDOWS UNOBSTRUCTED AS ADORNMENT AND A SOURCE OF NATURAL LIGHT.

(opposite) ANCHOR THE FOCUS OF A SMALL BEDROOM WITH STRONG VERTICAL
BEDPOSTS. A SUMPTUOUS TEXTILE WALL HANGING DRAPED OVER A WOODEN
HANGER THE WIDTH OF THE BED LEADS THE EYE TO THE FULL BREADTH OF THE
SPACE. MATCHING READING LAMPS AND PAIRED DRUM-SHAPED SEATS AT THE
FOOT OF THE BED FORM A UNIFIED FRAME.

EMPHASIZE THE STRONG HORIZONTALS OF A SHOJI SCREEN WITH VERTICAL QUILTING ON THE BEDCOVER AND THEN SOFTEN THEM WITH A RICH ALL-OVER PRINT OF A BED SKIRT. ROUNDED READING LAMPS ON ONE WALL AND THE CURVE OF THE CHAIR OPPOSITE COMPLETE THE BALANCE OF FORM.

Photo: Brady Architectural Photography / Design: Anjum Razvi and Brenda Lanza

Photo: Dominique Vorillon / Design: Lorcan O'Herlihy

(opposite) BALANCE BOLD, SHARP EDGES WITH ROUNDED FORMS TO SOFTEN THE EFFECT WITHOUT LESSENING THE IMPACT. HERE A ROUND SINK ON A CURVED GLASS COUNTER ACTS AS A FOIL FOR THE ANGULARITY OF THE STEPPED LEDGE AND MIRROR.

(above) A MASTER BATH IS TWICE AS FUNCTIONAL WITH DOUBLE SINKS. PERCH SINKS ON INDIVIDUAL STANDS TOPPED WITH THEIR OWN MIRRORS FOR A CLEAN, SYMMETRICAL LOOK. A TINY HORIZONTAL SLIT HIGH ON THE WALL LINKS THE SEPARATE WASHSTANDS AND, WITHOUT COMPROMISING PRIVACY, PROVIDES A GLIMPSE OF OUTDOOR BEAUTY WHILE ADMITTING NATURAL LIGHT.

Photo: Jacques Dirand / Design: Christian Liaigre

(above) MOUNT RODS ALONG AN INTERIOR WALL FOR HANGING ART AND ARTIFACTS. FLAT, WHITE PANELED WALLS AND A LONG DARK TRESTLE TABLE SET A SPARTAN TONE, COMPLEMENTED BY BLACK AND WHITE PRINTS OF PROPORTIONAL DIMENSIONS. INTERSPERSE UTILITARIAN OBJECTS HUNG VERTICALLY TO MAINTAIN THE STRENGTH OF THE RIGHT ANGLES WHILE SOFTENING THE EFFECT WITH THEIR IRREGULAR SHAPES.

(opposite) GIVE A RED LACQUERED ORIENTAL SCREEN NEW LIFE AS A HEADBOARD IN AN AIRY BEDROOM. COMPLETE THE BED FRAME WITH TWO SQUARE VANITY BENCHES UPHOLSTERED IN RED LEATHER AT THE FOOT OF THE BED, COMPLEMENTING THE SCREEN IN COLOR AND FORM.

Photo: davidduncanlivingston.com / Design: Kendel Wilkinson

Photo: Tim Street-Porter

harmony and balance

HARMONY AND BALANCE IS THE ESSENCE OF THE ANCIENT CHINESE PRACTICE OF *FENG SHUI*. Created to identify auspicious sites for burial, *Feng Shui* grew to include the placement of homes and business, and the items within them. Practitioners work with nature to establish balance for the optimal flow of energy. The elements—Fire, Water, Earth, Metal and Wood—are often incorporated into Eastern interiors, either symbolically or actually, and carefully interrelated to form a balanced universe.

BLEND EAST AND WEST STYLES TO CREATE BALANCE IN A PEACEFUL BEDROOM. DARK, GLEAMING ARTS AND CRAFTS COPPER LAMPS WITH BANDED MICA SHADES COMPLEMENT THE ROUGH TEXTURE OF THE INDIAN WOOD BEDSIDE TABLES AND TRUNK. A CHINESE SCREEN ANCHORS THE BEDROOM FURNISHINGS, EMANATING ENERGY AS WELL AS SERENITY.

yin and
yang

The Taoists attribute femininity or masculinity to all things. Yin, the feminine, includes things that are receptive, passive, round, dark, and cool. Mountains and plains are Yin. Yang, the masculine, is active. It includes straight lines, light colors, and warmth. Rivers and streams are Yang. Harmony, on any level, is achieved when Yin and Yang are in balance.

In home interiors, a balance of Yin and Yang is achieved in number of ways: Pair bold colors with subdued, neutral tones; warm colors with cool hues; sharp angles with soft curves; and textured surfaces with lustrous ones. Couple quilted upholstery and lush carpeting with lacquered wood and porcelain. Offset sharp angles with rounded pieces. Combine a richly textured sofa with the sheen of a Japanese *tansu*.

Photo: Courtesy of Brunschwig & Fils

(above) TO CONNOTE LUXURY AND WELL-BEING, ADD SMALL DOSES OF CHINESE LACQUER RED, SUCH AS IN THESE STRIPED PILLOWS, GLOSSY LAMP BASES, ORIENTAL RUG, DOLL AND BOOKS. BLACK LACQUER CHAIRS AND TABLES COMBINE WITH A SCREEN OF OVERSIZED CHINESE CHARACTERS TO UNIFY THE BLEND OF EAST AND WEST.

(opposite) ADD SPICE TO A FAMILIAR ARMCHAIR WITH A COLORFUL COTTON PRINT WITH AN EASTERN ACCENT. THIS TRADITIONAL CLUB CHAIR IS UPHOLSTERED IN A SUMPTUOUS PATTERN INSPIRED BY THAI FABRICS.

Photo: Chris A. Little / Design: Gandy/Peace, Inc.

Photo: Eric Roth / Design: Lloy Hack Associates

This contrast between Eastern and Western elements turns a beautiful room into an inspired, harmonious interior. ✐ Mix furniture upholstered with rich fabrics and patterns and a smooth pearwood cabinet, place celadon pottery near wicker furniture, or let Islamic calligraphy dance above a Georgian mantelpiece. ✐ Pile a sofa with a collection of pillows in bright silks and brocades in a monochromatic room. ✐ Position a modern, mid-twentieth century daybed with a low Chinese coffee table to create an irresistible resting spot.

Combine Eastern design elements with Western sensibilities to create points of interest in a balanced room. ✐ Stack a set of Chinese chests just below a hall mirror for a small still-life composition. ✐ Line a mantle with a row of Balinese smoked baskets.

(opposite) ENERGIZE YOUR LIVING ROOM WITH A BLEND OF EAST AND WEST—A STRIPPED AND POLISHED CHINESE CHEST AND SEATING INSPIRED BY MIES VAN DER ROHE'S BARCELONA FURNITURE. ACCENT LIGHTING EMPHASIZES THE SIMPLE FORM AND GOLDEN WOOD TONES OF THE CHEST, WHICH COMPLEMENT THE CREAM-COLORED LEATHER UPHOLSTERY OF THE SEATING.

(top left) WITH AN ECLECTIC MIX OF FURNISHINGS, UNIFY THE ROOM WITH A FOCAL PIECE. A CHINESE BAMBOO COAT MOUNTED ON A CHERRY ROD UNIFIES THE TEXTURES AND NATURAL TONES IN THIS SITTING AREA.

(bottom left) EAST MEETS WEST ATOP A CLASSIC, CARVED MANTEL. A COLORFUL PARADE OF PAKISTANI FIGURINES ECHOES THE HUES AND SHAPES OF THE ISLAMIC SCRIPT AND FLOWER FORMS OF THE ARTWORK ABOVE.

Photo: John Sutton / Design: Dan Phipps

(above) BALANCE YIN AND YANG BY PAIRING SPARE, RECTILINEAR ARCHITECTURE
WITH DECORATIVE PIECES FROM THE EAST, SUCH AS THESE CARVED SCULPTURES.
CREAMY WHITE WALLS, CONCRETE FLOORS, AND STEEL MANTEL.

(left) INTRODUCE AN ANTIQUE JAPANESE TANSU TO LEND CLEAN LINES AND
VALUABLE STORAGE SPACE TO A WESTERN ROOM. THIS PIECE HEIGHTENS THE
INTERPLAY BETWEEN THE WARM TONES OF THE PINE FLOORS AND THE DEEP
GREEN WALLS.

(opposite) COMPOSE A SUBTLY BALANCED EAST-WEST DÈCOR WITH A MIX OF LIGHT
AND DARK, ROUGH AND SMOOTH. HIGHLIGHT WESTERN STEMWARE IN AN
ILLUMINATED GLASS-FRONT CABINET TO BALANCE A DINING AREA RICH IN NATURAL
WOOD AND WALLPAPERED IN RAW SILK. THE SHEEN, ECHOED IN A GILT ACCENT IN
AN OPPOSITE CORNER AND A VIBRANT WHITE FLORAL CENTERPIECE, ENLIVENS THE
RICH TEXTURAL DÉCOR. INTRODUCE DARK COLORS IN SMALL DOSES TO GIVE LIFE
TO THE NEUTRAL TONES.

Photo: Peter Jaquith / Design: Barbara Colman

Photo: Douglas Salin
Lighting Design: Michael Souter
Design: Bob Miller, Flegels

Photo: Matthew Millman / Design: Dianna Wong

Photo: www.davidduncanlivingston.com / Design: McDonald & Moore / Architecture: Duncan Todd

(opposite) ADD A SUBTLE EASTERN NOTE TO A WESTERN LIVING ROOM WITH A

MIX OF TEXTURES AND FORMS LINKED BY A STYLIZED FIREPLACE SURROUND.

ACCENT WITH SILK TASSELS AND DELICATE POTTED PLANTS.

(above) PLACE A COROMANDEL SCREEN BEHIND THE SOFA TO DIVERT THE EYE

FROM AN EXPANSE OF VAULTED CEILING WITHOUT DIMINISHING ITS POWER. THE

ZIGZAG LINE OF THE SCREEN COMPLEMENTS THE ANGLES OF THE

ARCHITECTURE WHILE ITS RICH TONES AND FLUID DESIGN EASE THEIR EFFECT.

IMITATE THE JAPANESE AFFINITY FOR SIMPLICITY WITH CLASSIC CONTEMPORARY FURNISHINGS POSITIONED FOR FUNCTION AND SYMMETRY. SANDBLASTED BLACK MARBLE FLOORING PROVIDES A RICH TEXTURED GROUND FOR THE MIX OF LINEN AND LEATHER UPHOLSTERY. OFFSET ANGULAR FURNISHINGS WITH THE SWEEPING ARC OF A FLOOR LAMP. LET DAYLIGHT FLOOD THE ROOM THROUGH UNADORNED WINDOWS TO MAKE THE NEUTRAL PALETTE COME ALIVE.

Photo: Nick Wheeler / Design: Peter Forbes

Photo: Alan Weintraub / Design: Fu Tung Cheng

(above) INTRODUCE A HORIZONTAL SHOCK OF WATERY BLUE TO REDUCE THE IMPACT OF A LOW CEILING. A STAND OF BAMBOO VIEWED THROUGH THE LONG, LOW WINDOW LINKS THE COLORS AND ADDS A DECIDEDLY EASTERN ELEMENT.

(opposite) VARY KITCHEN COUNTER HEIGHTS AND MATERIALS FOR A BOLD LOOK. LINK THE ROUGH-HEWN SURFACE OF A SLATE BACKSPLASH AND THE HIGH GLOSS FINISH OF A WOOD COUNTERTOP WITH A CAST CONCRETE COUNTERTOP OF RICH EARTHY GRAY. FLAT FRONT CABINETRY PROVIDES THE UNADORNED BACKDROP TO MAXIMIZE THE IMPACT OF THE DIVERSE TEXTURES AND THE ANGLES THEY FORM.

CARVE OUT A SERENE READING NOOK IN A CORNER OF YOUR LIVING ROOM. POSITION AN UNCOMPLICATED CHAISE IN FRONT OF UNADORNED WINDOWS TO TAKE ADVANTAGE OF NATURAL LIGHT (AND AN AWE-INSPIRING VIEW IN THIS CASE). PILE ON PILLOWS IN EXOTIC, SILKY PRINTS AND SUSPEND SMALL JAPANESE LANTERNS OVERHEAD FOR EAST-WEST ELAN.

Photo: Tim Street-Porter

(opposite) MAINTAIN HARMONIOUS LOOK WHILE PROVIDING DISTINCTION BETWEEN SLEEPING

AND SITTING AREAS WITH SHOJI-LIKE TRANSLUCENT PANELS. FURTHER UNITE THE LOOK WITH A

MUTED COLOR PALETTE THROUGH-OUT, CONTRASTING TEXTURES-A LUSTROUS PRINT DUVET

COVER AND SOFT VELVET CHAIR UPHOLSTERY.

(above) CREATE A RESTFUL BEDROOM WITH MUTED TONES FOR WALLS AND CARPET. A LOW

PLATFORM BED TAKES ON STATURE WHEN COVERED IN A SUBTLY LUSTROUS PRINT WITHIN THE

ROOM'S PALETTE. USE BEDSIDE LAMPS TO SPOTLIGHT LINEAR ARTWORK AND A JAPANESE TEA

TRAY FOR AN INVITING EAST-WEST LOOK.

(above) TURN A SUNNY BAY WINDOW INTO A JAPANESE GARDEN. LET SMOOTH STONES CONNOTE

A RIVER; LARGER ROCKS AND POTTED SPIDER PLANTS REPRESENT THE GRASSY BANKS. TALL

BAMBOO AND POTTED PALMS BECOME TREES. EARTHENWARE URNS AND ARTIFACTS WITH AN

ASIAN THEME ACT AS A THRESHOLD BETWEEN THIS EXOTIC INSTALLATION AND THE ADJACENT

LIVING AREA.

(above) INTEGRATE THE NATURAL COLORS AND TEXTURES VIEWED THROUGH FLOOR-TO-

CEILING WINDOWS INTO THE SURFACES OF YOUR BATH. RETRACTABLE SHOJI SCREENS ALLOW

PRIVACY WHEN NEEDED AND BAMBOO SHADES STRIKE A COMPROMISE FOR THE TIMES WHEN

DAPPLED LIGHT IS PREFERABLE IN THE BATH AND PRIVACY IS NOT AN ISSUE.

LET A BAMBOO SHADE FILTER LIGHT INTO A BEDROOM FULL OF EASTERN TEXTURES AND PATTERNS FOR A HARMONIOUS, RESTFUL AMBIANCE. A LUSTROUS GOLD PILLOW AMIDST THE COLLECTION ON THE BED INTEGRATES THE GILT EDGES OF THE SCREEN WITH THE NATURAL TEXTURES IN THE ROOM FOR A HARMONIOUS BLEND OF EAST AND WEST.

Photo: Bill Rothschild / Design: Yvette Gervey

Photo: www.davidduncanlivingston.com / Design: Your Space

Photo: William Waldron / Design: John F. Saladino

(opposite) DRESS A HONEY COLORED PLATFORM BED WITH LUSH BUT CASUAL NATURAL LINENS TO WARM CONCRETE ARCHITECTURAL ELEMENTS AND INTRODUCE AN EASTERN LOOK. HANG COLORFUL ARTWORK TO ENLIVEN A WHITE ROOM. THIS FLAMING RED SUN ADDS HEAT AND ENERGY WITH ITS SYMBOLIC EASTERN GLOW. A PLUSH RUG WELCOMES BARE FEET ON CHILLY MORNINGS.

(above) SET OFF THE SIMPLE COLORS OF A 17TH CENTURY JAPANESE SCREEN WITH AN ANTIQUE CHEST OF SIMILAR PROPORTION TO CREATE A FOCAL POINT IN THE LIVING ROOM. THE STYLIZED JAPANESE PAINTING COMBINES WITH THE ELABORATE DECORATION OF THE CHEST TO CREATE AN EXQUISITE EAST-WEST BLEND.

Photo: Steve Vierra / Design: Growing Spaces

(above) OFFSET A DARK ASIAN SCREEN WITH A MAHOGANY CHAIR UPHOLSTERED IN A SILK PRINT OF CHINESE RED ON A NEUTRAL GROUND. THE GILT DETAIL OF THE CHAIR LINKS THE TWO AND ENHANCES THE OPULENCE OF THIS EAST-WEST LOOK.

(opposite) HANG A KIMONO OVER A DARK MISSION OAK FIREPLACE AS A CONTRASTING CENTRAL PIECE IN A COLOR SCHEME OF MUTED GRAYS. AN AIRY CUTOUT WOODCARVING SUSPENDED FROM A BEAM REPEATS THE DARK TONES AND DRAWS THE FOCUS DOWN FROM THE SOARING CEILINGS. THE ROOM RETAINS ITS SPACIOUS FEELING WITHOUT THE CHILL OF EXPANSIVE WHITE SPACE.

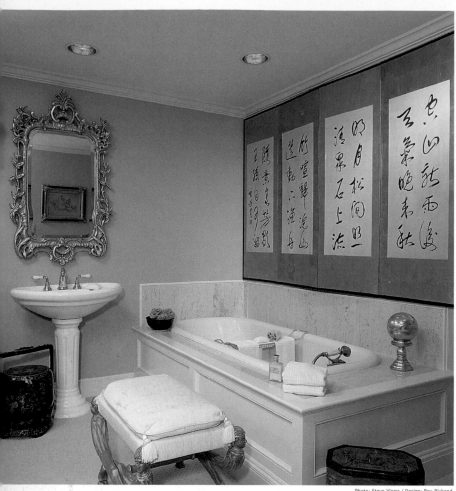

(above) HANG A DECORATIVE SCREEN OF ASIAN CALLIGRAPHY TO TRANSFORM A CLASSIC WESTERN BATHROOM INTO A BLEND OF EAST AND WEST.

(opposite) FOR A FEMININE BATHROOM MERGE THE BEST OF EAST AND WEST WITH EXPANSIVE TILE COUNTERS TOPPING WHITE VANITIES AND A TRADITIONAL CHINESE, RICHLY ORNAMENTED PORCELAIN STOOL. DRESS THE WINDOW WITH A FAN-SHAPED SWATH OF PINK SILK.

Photo: Grey Crawford / Design: Kelly Wearstler

color and
texture

THE USE OF COLOR IN EASTERN CULTURES RANGES FROM THE
JAPANESE AFFINITY FOR EARTHY, NEUTRAL TONES, OFTEN
COMPLEMENTED WITH A BURST OF BOLD CLEAR PIGMENT, TO
THE COMPLICATED INTERMINGLED HUES AND TONES FOUND IN
PERSIAN CARPETS AND INDIAN BROCADES.

Ancient Eastern beliefs include much color symbolism that
relates to the emotional responses the colors evoke. Modern-day
science has corroborated what the ancients may have instinctively
known. The Chinese five-color theory, a component of the practice
of *Feng Shui*, associates a color with each of the five elements. Red,
the color of fire, is considered auspicious. Science has determined
that red invigorates and excites. Blue, the color of water, connotes
spirituality. Blue soothes and cools. Green, the color of wood,
indicates exuberant growth. It is uplifting and warm. Yellow, the
color of earth, connotes wealth and power. Westerner's know it to
be a color of contentment and harmony. White, the color of metal,
is the color of fulfillment. White takes on different aspects
depending upon its surrounding colors.

**SILVER LEAF FURNITURE SETS AN OPULENT TONE. PAIR IT WITH SILKY FABRICS AND A WARM COLOR PALETTE
FOR AN EXOTIC YET INVITING LOOK.**

palette and
pattern

When you choose your colors, think of the responses they trigger. Keep in mind that combining colors introduces multiple attributes. Red can work in a bedroom, for example, if paired with a sufficient amount of a restful tone to quiet its effect.

  ✐ Add a bold splash of color to enliven a neutral palette. ✐ Use the Japanese tradition of monochromatic schemes and explore all values within a range. Add interest with pattern and texture. ✐ Evoke the mystique of India with brilliant colors in dazzling jewel tones.

  The Eastern affinity for natural fibers and materials introduces a broad range of textures. Woven natural fabrics, bamboo, lacquered wood, rice paper lanterns, sea grass carpets, linen, brocade, velvet, and raw silk all lend themselves to the East-West style.

  A variety of textures adds dimension to a monochromatic scheme. A sleek silk shantung pillow sham may be all that's needed to enliven a bedroom done in a single color. A crinkly unbleached cotton duvet cover can turn a stark bedroom into an inviting, cozy nook. With a palette of bold colors, let texture quiet the effect. Soft velvets or the rough texture of sea grass can tone down a vibrant hue.

  Don't ignore the textural effect of woods and porcelains. A shiny lacquered wood chest has a more enlivening effect than a rough, rustic one. A porcelain vase will gleam in a corner where an earthenware jug would quietly anchor the spot.

  Where complementary bold colors are used, match textures and patterns so the difference in the colors is the focal point. Where colors are similar or alike, vary textures wildly—a matelassé coverlet with embroidered, silky pillows, lacy white shams on a linen spread, sheer drapery against a concrete wall.

Photo: Paul Ferrino / Design: Peter Forbes

(above) USE COLOR AND TEXTURE TO SUBTLY UNIFY SEPARATE FUNCTIONAL AREAS OF AN OPEN FLOOR PLAN. THE ROYAL BLUE DINING ROOM CHAIRS ARE ECHOED IN THROW PILLOWS ON THE LIVING AREA SOFA. THE DARK EARTHEN TABLEWARE IS AKIN TO THE STONE FIREPLACE BEYOND.

(right) CHOOSE A GARDEN GATE OF WOOD SLATS AND STAINLESS STEEL TO ACT AS AN INTERESTING INTRODUCTION TO AN EAST-WEST HOME. THE SIMPLICITY OF LINE AND STRIKING JUXTAPOSITION OF MATERIALS MAKES A POWERFUL STATEMENT.

Photo: Luis Ferreira Alves / Architecture: Eduardo Souto Moura

CAPTURE THE EASTERN FEEL WITH A BOLD COLOR
SPLASH IN A NEUTRAL ROOM. SCULPTURAL
FURNISHINGS IN RICH ORANGE TONES SEEM TO FLOAT
IN A ROOM WITH UNADORNED WHITE WALLS AND
WINDOW TREATMENT. THE ROOM RADIATES AN
INVITATION TO SIT A WHILE.

Photo: Bjorg Arnarsdottir / Architect: Kar Ho Architect

(above) UPHOLSTER A CHAISE IN PEARLY GRAY SILK SHANTUNG BORDERED IN

SILK CORDING AND ACCENTED WITH TASSELS FOR A LOOK OF COOL

SOPHISTICATION. AN ASIAN LACQUERED CHEST AND SLEEK HARDWOOD

FLOORING MATCH THE SHEEN AND ADD DENSITY. SOFTEN THE EFFECT BY

FILTERING DAYLIGHT THROUGH BAMBOO SHADES.

(opposite) LAYER WHITE ON WHITE IN EMBROIDERED FLORAL MOTIFS AND

NUBBY RIBBING TO ADD DEPTH TO A PRISTINE BEDROOM. NATURAL LIGHT

FILTERED THROUGH TRANSLUCENT SHOJI-LIKE SCREENS AND WOODEN SLATTED

BLINDS GIVES THE ROOM A WARM GLOW.

Photo: Peter Margonelli / Interior Design: Benjamin Noriega-Ortiz

(above) USE BOLD COLORS FOR WALLS AS A BACKDROP FOR MINIMAL
APPOINTMENTS. HERE THE ELEGANT ORCHID DISPLAYED ON A GLASS-TOPPED TABLE
IS ALL THE ADORNMENT NECESSARY FOR THIS COLORFUL APARTMENT PALETTE.
EVEN WITH BOLD COLORS, SERENITY PREVAILS.

(right) TRANSFORM A SMALL BEDROOM INTO A REGAL EASTERN DELIGHT WITH
STRONG COLORS AND RICH FABRICS. SAFFRON, THE COLOR OF MONKS' ROBES,
PAIRED WITH MOST AUSPICIOUS DEEP RED CALLS FOR LUSTROUS BROCADES AND
SILKS. HIGHLY POLISHED WOOD FURNISHINGS AND CANDLELIGHT COMPLETE THE
OPULENT LOOK.

Photo and Design: Charlotte Jensen

(above) PAINT WALLS A DEEP, RICH RED FOR AN INSTANT EASTERN EFFECT.
BLACK LACQUERED FURNISHINGS ECHO THE SHEEN OF THE SATIN FINISHED
WALLS WHILE TRANSLUCENT SHOJI SCREENS KEEP THE GLOW FROM
OVERWHELMING.

(opposite) USE SLATE TILES FOR A RICH BACK SPLASH. TINY INLAID STONE
DETAIL ADDS A SUBTLE NOTE. GIVE THE RANGE HOOD A THIN COAT OF HONEY
COLORED PLASTER TO RELIEVE THE DARK PURPLISH-BLUE OF THE SLATE.
ABSTRACT DRAWINGS CUT INTO THE PLASTER AS IT DRIES TRANSFORMS AN
UTILITARIAN SURFACE INTO ART. THE ROUGH NATURAL SURFACES ARE GIVEN
ADDED LIFE AS THEY GLINT OFF THE STAINLESS STEEL COUNTERTOP.

Photo: Mark Cohen / Design: Fu Tung Cheng

Photo: Peter Margonelli / Interior Design: Benjamin Noriega-Ortiz

Photo: Dorothy Perry / Design: Tangee Harris-Prichett

(above) IN A SITTING AREA WITH AN ECLECTIC MIX OF FURNISHINGS, PROVIDE COHESION THROUGH COLOR AND TEXTURE. A BRIGHTLY COLORED WOOL RUG GROUNDS THE OTHERWISE NEUTRAL COLOR SCHEME, WHILE AN EAMES SOFA AND A NOGUCHI COFFEE TABLE PROVIDE SMOOTH LINES AND SLEEK SURFACES. THE WICKER CHAIRS AND SLATTED BLINDS GIVE THE ROOM AN AIRY LIGHT-FILLED LOOK.

(left) HANG A BAMBOO SHADE AT THE HEAD OF A SIMPLE PLATFORM BED FOR DEFINITION AND AS A VISUAL LINK TO TATAMI MATS USED AS CARPETING. TRY LUSH ULTRASUEDE BEDCOVERS IN RICH OCHRE AS A TEXTURAL COUNTERPOINT. SHOJI SCREENS LIGHTEN AND RELIEVE THE MONOCHROMATIC COLOR SCHEME.

(opposite) CHOOSE WARM EARTH TONES FOR A SENSUOUS BEDROOM. PAIR THE ROUGH TEXTURES OF WOOD AND LEATHER NATIVE AMERICAN ART WITH SOFTLY RIBBED CHENILLE ON A FUTON FOR EAST-WEST IMPACT AND TACTILE DELIGHT.

Photo: Peter Jaquith / Interior Design: Barbara Colman

Photo: Tim Lee / Interior Design: Ho Sang Shin, Antine Associates

(opposite) USE CALMING JADE TONES FOR DOMINANT COLOR TO CREATE A RESTFUL BEDROOM.
THE BED, A PLATFORM UPHOLSTERED IN JADE GREEN, IS DRESSED WITH BLANKETS AND
PILLOWS IN NEUTRAL TONES. THE FLORAL PILLOWCASES AGAINST THE STRIPED SHAMS ADD
INTEREST AND ARE GROUNDED BY THE TEXTURE OF THE BLANKET. BAMBOO SHADES CREATE
AN AURA OF THE EAST. GREEN BORDERS FOR TOP SHEET AND ACCENT PILLOW CREATE UNITY
OF COLOR WITHIN THIS TEXTURAL MEDLEY.

(above) USE ANALOGOUS COLORS IN SHIMMERING FABRICS. JUXTAPOSE GREEN AND ORANGE,
LINKED BY THEIR SHARED YELLOW COMPONENT, FOR A BOLD COLOR STATEMENT. IDENTICAL
FABRICS KEEP THE COLOR SCHEME FROM BECOMING OVERPOWERING. THE SILKY SHEEN AND
STRAIGHTFORWARD PATTERN ADD STABILITY.

Photo: Alan Weintraub / Design: Barry Brukoff

(above) TAKE ADVANTAGE OF THE BEAUTY AND PRACTICALITY OF SLATE FLOOR TILES IN THE ENTRYWAY. STIPPLE-PAINT WALLS IN A COPPERY TONE FOUND IN THE VARIEGATED SLATE TO GIVE THE AREA A WELCOMING, EARTHY GLOW.

(opposite) COLOR AND TEXTURE ARE ALMOST INSEPARABLE IN VARIEGATED SLATE TILES. ACCENTUATE THE RICH GOLDEN TONES WITH LIMESTONE FLOOR TILING AND PUNCTUATE WITH A NATURAL CHERRY WASHSTAND. RAFFIA MATS SUBTLY ADD TO THE OUTDOOR APPEAL OF THIS BATH.

Photo: Jeff McNamara / Design: Austin Patterson Disston

Photo: Ira Nowinski / Design: Levitt/Weaver

(opposite) ACHIEVE A TRANQUIL LOOK IN THE BATHROOM WITH THE MUTING EFFECT OF
UNPOLISHED STONE FOR COUNTERS AND TUB SURROUND. PAIRED WITH RUSTIC WOOD THE
LOOK IS SIMPLE AND NATURAL. WHITE PORCELAIN FIXTURES AND WHITE WALLS CONTRAST
WITH THE DARK ELEMENTS AND GIVE THE ROOM ITS CLEAN, FRESH FEELING.

(above) FACE A SHOWER WALL WITH CAST ROCK TO CAPTURE THE ESSENCE OF BATHING IN A
MOUNTAIN STREAM. AWASH IN NATURAL LIGHT, THE TEXTURED SURFACE TAKES ON ADDED
DEPTH AND GIVES THE ROOM A FRESH AIR FEELING. A CONCRETE TUB SURROUND
COMPLEMENTS THE WALL TREATMENT AND ADDS TO THE AURA.

Photo: Scott Frances / Design: Brett Beldock

(left) GIVE YOUR ROOM POSITIVE ENERGY, WARMTH, AND VITALITY WITH BOLD RED. HERE UPHOLSTERY FABRIC REMINISCENT OF CHINESE PEONIES CALMS THE RED WITH ITS GOLD BACKGROUND.

(opposite above) CHOOSE BAMBOO FURNISHINGS TO TONE DOWN THE AUSTERITY OF DARK BEAMS. INTRODUCE THE TEXTURES OF RAW SILK AND TAPESTRY FOR A RICH MIXTURE IN NATURAL TONES.

(opposite bottom) CREATE AN ETHEREAL SLEEPING SPACE WITH A CANOPY BED CARVED IN AN EASTERN STYLE. A BOLD BUT RESTFUL SILK-SCREENED RED BEDCOVER BALANCES A GOSSAMER DRAPERY FOR THE PERFECT BLEND OF AIRY AND GROUNDED. THE OUTDOOR FEEL OF THIS SLEEPING PORCH CAN BE DUPLICATED INDOORS WITH TEXTURAL NATURAL WINDOW TREATMENTS AND POTTED GREENERY.

Photo: Eric Roth

Photo: Tim Street-Porter

Photo: Steve Vierra / Design: Marian Glasgow

(opposite) USE SAFFRON GOLD TO INFUSE A REGAL EASTERN NOTE. THIS EXOTIC PRINT INTRODUCES A COMPLEMENTARY VIOLET TONE AND GIVES UPHOLSTERED BANQUE SEATING AN ELEGANT AIR.

(above) USE RED, THE MOST AUSPICIOUS COLOR ACCORDING TO ANCIENT CHINESE WISDOM, FOR A ROOM THAT INSTANTLY EXCITES AND ENLIVENS. A DEEP TONE IN SATIN FINISH BECOMES AN ELEGANT BACKDROP WITH AN EASTERN FEEL.

SOFTEN THE ROUGH-HEWN TEXTURES OF ARCHITECTURAL ELEMENTS WITH NATURAL
COTTON BEDDING AND GOSSAMER WHITE DRAPERY FOR AN APPEALING BEDROOM.
TRANSLUCENT SLIDING CLOSET DOORS INTRODUCE FILTERED LIGHT AND DESIGN
APPEAL WHILE SERVING TO CONCEAL CLOSET CLUTTER.

Photo: David Glomb / Design: Insight West (Goers and Williamson)

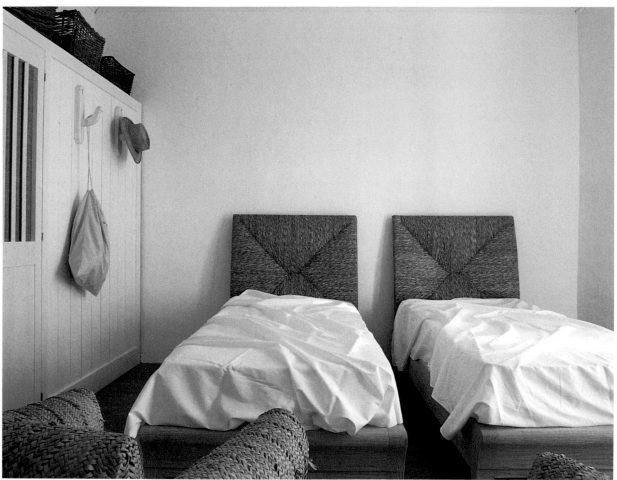

Photo: Jacques Dirand / Design: Christian Liaigre

Photo: Bill Rothschild / Design: Gold & Genauer Associated

(opposite) INTRODUCE AN EASTERN TOUCH WITH A RICE PAPER LANTERN TO ILLUMINATE A
MULTICULTURAL COMPOSITION ON A SIDE TABLE.

(above) GIVE AN 18TH CENTURY JAPANESE SCREEN THE OPTIMAL VIEWING SPOT. LET ITS
BRILLIANT COLORS AND ETHEREAL STYLE DICTATE AN UNDERSTATED DÉCOR.

Photo: Bill Rothschild / Design: Yvette Gervey

Photo: Eric Zepeda / Interior Design: Charles Falls / Lighting Design: Robert Truax and Kenton Knapp

Photo and Lighting Design: Randall Whitehead / Interior Design: Christian Wright and Gerald Simpkins

(opposite) CREATE A CEREMONIAL ROOM TO DISPLAY EASTERN TREASURES. A
LUXURIOUS SILK KIMONO SERVES AS ART WHEN DRAPED OVER A ROD. MINIATURE
REPLICAS OF SHRINES ADD A SPIRITUAL ELEMENT WHEN SUSPENDED FROM THE
CEILING AND LIT FROM WITHIN. A LOW TABLE CAN BE PREPARED FOR A RITUAL TEA
WITH JAPANESE STONEWARE, CANDLES, AND FLOOR MAT FOR SEATING.

(above) LET GEISHA FIGURINES GRACE A DINING TABLE DRESSED WITH A SILK
BROCADE RUNNER—FAR MORE DECORATIVE THAN IF CONFINED TO A DISPLAY
CABINET.

(right) USE A BLUE FILTER ON ACCENT LIGHTING TO GIVE A SIMPLE CELADON VASE
MAJESTIC PRESENCE.

Photo: Tim Street-Porter / Design: Jeffry Weisman

(above) SOFTEN YOUR CONTEMPORARY LIVING ROOM WITH A JAPANESE SILK SCREEN. A VASE
OF FRESH CHERRY BLOSSOMS TO MATCH THOSE IN THE SCREEN DRAWS THE PEACEFUL AURA
FURTHER INTO THE ROOM.

(opposite) IN A SERENE NEUTRAL DINING AREA WITH A CHINESE CARPET UNDERFOOT, LET A
DELICATE CHINESE PORCELAIN BOWL ACT ALONE AS CENTERPIECE.

Photo: Eric Oxendorf / Interior Design: Bill Manly / Lighting Design: Stephen Klein

Photo: Grey Crawford / Design: Kelly Wearstler

(above) A CANE AND WOOD TELEVISION CABINET BECOMES A GATEWAY TO A JAPANESE
GARDEN WHEN BACKED WITH AN EVOCATIVE CHERRY BLOSSOM MURAL.

(opposite) LET A JAPANESE SCROLL DICTATE THE COLOR SCHEME AND SET THE MOOD FOR
YOUR LIVING ROOM. GIVE IT CENTRAL POSITION ABOVE THE FIREPLACE. THE MUTED
COLORS REPEATED IN THE UPHOLSTERY AND CARPET LEND AN ETHEREAL QUALITY TO THIS
DÈCOR.

(above) ADD A GRACEFUL LINE TO A DECORATIVE ASIAN CHEST WITH SCULPTURED STORKS, WHICH FIGURE PROMINENTLY IN JAPANESE MYTHOLOGY.

(opposite) COMPLEMENT THE MUTED EARTHY COLOR SCHEME OF A RESTFUL SITTING AREA WITH A CALLIGRAPHIC WALL PLAQUE IN RICH WOOD TONES.

Photo: Bill Rothschild / Design: Patricia Bonis

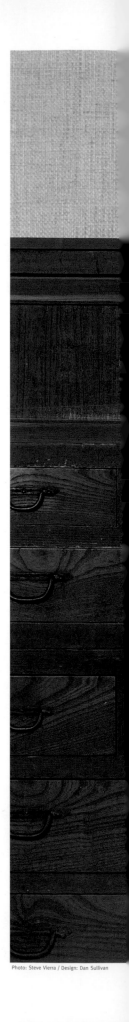

(above) POTTED HERBS NEED NOT BE RELEGATED TO THE KITCHEN WINDOWSILL. DRESS ONE UP IN A CELADON CACHEPOT AND PLACE IT ON A DELICATELY DECORATED CHINESE TABLE FOR AN EXOTIC ACCENT IN THE LIVING ROOM.

(opposite) ADD A SURPRISING ACCENT TO A LARGE JAPANESE TANSU. SET AN EXOTIC PAPIER MACHÉ DRAGON MASK ON AN OPEN DRAWER TO INCREASE ITS IMPACT BY INTERRUPTING THE SOLID WOOD OF THE CHEST. SET A SIMPLE COLOR PRINT ON TOP TO LIGHTEN THE MOOD WHILE INTRODUCING A WESTERN ELEMENT.

Photo: Steve Vierra / Design: Dan Sullivan

Photo: Dennis Anderson / Interior Design: Randall Whitehead / Lighting Design: Randall Whitehead and Catherine Ng

(above) ELEVATE INDIVIDUAL PIECES IN A DISPLAY OF CERAMICS. PLACE SMALLEST PIECES ON THE HIGHEST PEDESTALS FOR VISUAL BALANCE.

(opposite) GET COLOR INSPIRATION FROM A DECORATIVE CHINESE TRAY TABLE. THE SUBDUED MAROON OF THESE WALLS FITS THE CLASSIC WESTERN ARCHITECTURE WHILE THE EXQUISITE TABLE, ASSISTED BY A RICE PAPER LAMP, ADDS AN ELEMENT OF THE EAST.

Photo: Bill Rothschild / Design: Teri Seidman

Photo: Dennis Anderson / Interior Design: Jessica Hall & Associates / Lighting Design: Randall Whitehead and Catherine Ng

(opposite) PRESENT AN EASTERN DINING EXPERIENCE WITH FINE PORCELAIN SET ON A RED
LACQUERED TRAY. A WOVEN TABLE RUNNER IN A RICH DARK TONE CALMS THE BRIGHT
COLORS AND ADDS TEXTURAL BALANCE.

(above) SITTING BUDDHAS SEEM TO LEVITATE WHEN DISPLAYED ON TRANSPARENT STANDS.
GET TWICE THE EFFECT BY PLACING THEM WHERE THEY WILL REFLECT IN A WINDOW AT
NIGHT.

ABC Carpet and Home
881 & 888 Broadway at E. 19th Street
New York, NY 10003
212.473.3000

777 South Congress
Delray Beach, Florida
561.279.7777

The Source
1504 Old Country Road
Westbury, Long Island
516.222.1113

ABC Carpet at Harrods
Knightsbridge, London
44.171.730.1234

Albert Langdon, Inc.
126 Charles Street
Boston, MA 02114
617.523.5954

Algabar
920 North La Cienega Boulevard
West Hollywood, CA 90069
310.360.3500

Anthropologie
1.800.309.2500
www.anthropologie.com

Artemis
139 Newbury Street
Boston, MA 02116
617.867.0900

Big Pagoda Company
1903 Fillmore Street
San Francisco, CA 94115
415.563.8727
www.bigpagoda.com

Dandelion
55 Potrero Avenue
San Francisco, CA 94103
415.436.9500
www.dandeliononline.com

Dosa
107 Thompson Street
New York, NY 10012
800.995.3672

Evelyn's Antique Chinese Furniture
381 Hayes Street
San Francisco, CA 94102
415.255.1815

Judith Dowling Asian Art
133 Charles Street
Boston, MA 02114
617.523.5211

Mohr&McPherson
290 Concord Avenue
Cambridge, MA 02138
617.354.6662

81 Arlington Street
Boston, MA 02116
617.338.1288

463 Fore Street
Portland, ME 04101
207.871.1868

Pier One
461 Fifth Avenue
New York, NY 10017
1.800.447.4371
www.pier1.com

Portico Home
72 Spring Street
New York, NY 10012
212.941.7800

Shi
233 Elizabeth Street
(Between Prince and Houston Streets)
New York, NY 10012
212.334.4330

Smith and Hawken
1.800.940.1170
www.smithandhawken.com

Takashimaya
693 Fifth Avenue
New York, NY 10022
1.800.753.2038

Antine Associates, Inc.
1028 Arcadian Way
Fort Lee, NJ 07024

Austin Patterson Disston Architects, LLC
376 Pequot Avenue
Southport, CT 06490

Thomas M. Beeton, Inc.
723 Ω North La Cienega Boulevard
Los Angeles, CA 90069

Brett Beldock
Brett Design Inc.
201 East 87th Street
New York, NY

Hagy Belzberg
Belzbeg Architects
9615 Brighton Way
Beverly Hills, CA 90210

Patricia Bonis Interiors, Inc.
8 Fairway Court
Cresskill, NJ 07626

Barry Brukoff

Brukoff Design Associates
480 Gate Five Road
Sausalito, CA 94965

Brunschwig & Fils
979 Third Avenue
New York, NY 10022

Carla Carstensí Designs
1 Timber View Road
Soquel, CA 95073

Fu Tung Cheng
Cheng Design
2808 San Pablo Avenue
Berkeley, CA 94702

Barbara Colman
Covington/Colman
14 Imperial Place
Providence, RI 02903

Marcia Connors
Growing Spaces
4 Fall Lane
Canton, MA 02021

Orlando Diaz-Azcuy Designs
45 Maiden Lane
San Francisco, CA 94108

Charles Falls
(deceased)

Linda Ferry
Architectural Illumination
P.O. Box 2690
Monterey, CA 93942

Peter Forbes and Associates
70 Long Wharf
Boston, MA 02110

Becca Foster Lighting Design
522 Second Street
San Francisco, CA 94107

Gandy/Peace, Inc.
3195 Paces Ferry Place
Atlanta, GA 30305

Yvette B. Gervey Interiors, Inc.
14 West 75th Street
New York, NY 10023

Marian Glasgow Interiors
9 Laurel Street
Newton Centre, MA 01776

Gold & Genauer Associated
515 East 72nd Street
New York, NY 10021

Growing Spaces
4 Fall Lane
Canton, MA 02021

Lloy Hack Associates
425 Boylston Street
Boston, MA 02116

Jessica Hall & Associates
1301 6th Street, Suite G
San Francisco, CA 94107

Tangee Harris-Prichett
Tangee Inc.
5306 South Hyde Park Boulevard
Chicago, IL 60615

Michael Helm
200 7th Avenue, #110
Santa Cruz, CA 95062

Kar Ho Architect
117 West 17th Street
New York, NY 10011

Insight West
Bruce Goers, Wayne Williamson &
Sam Cardella
45-125 Panorama Drive
Palm Desert, CA 92260

Charlotte Jensen
11464 Escoba Place
San Diego, CA 92127

Raymond Joseph Design
1901 West Race Street
Chicago, IL 60622

Cheryl Kinay
92 Forest Avenue
Locust Valley, NY 11560

Steven L. Klein
Standard Electric Supply Co.
222 North Emmber Lane
Milwaukee, WI 53233

Kenton Knapp Design
P.O. Box 2498
Santa Cruz, CA 95063

Brenda Lanza
13279 Vinter Way
Poway, CA 92064

Kelley Lasser
2955 Clay Street #2
San Francisco, CA 94123

Christian Liaigre
61 rue de Varenne
Paris, France 75007

Lightolier
631 Airport Road
Fall River, MA 02720

Luminaire
301 West Superior Street
Chicago, IL 60610

Machine-Age Corporation
354 Congress Street
Boston, MA 02210

William Manly Associates, Inc.
301 North Water Street
Milwaukee, WI 53201

William David Martin and Associates
P.O. Box 2053
Monterey, CA 93940

Rick Mather Architects
123 Camden High Street
London NW1 7JR England

Donald Maxcy Design Associates
439 Webster Street
Monterey, CA 93940

McDonald & Moore Ltd.
20 N. Almaden Avenue
San Jose, CA 95110

Bob Miller
Flegels
870 Santa Cruz Avenue
Menlo Park, CA 94025

The Morson Collection
100 E. Walton Street
Chicago, IL 60611

Catherine Ng
1246 28th Street
San Francisco, CA 94107

Benjamin Noriega-Ortiz
75 Spring Street
New York, NY 10012

Sandra Nunnerly, Inc.
112 E. 71st Street
New York, NY 10021

Lorcan OíHerlihy
Dan Phipps and Associates
131 Post Street
San Francisco, CA 94109

Poliform USA, Inc.
150 East 58th Street, Floor 9
New York, NY 10155

Anjum Razvi
14829 Pensaquitos Court
San Diego, CA 92129

Buddy Rhodes
2130 Oakdale Avenue
San Francisco, CA 94124

Roche Bobois USA
183 Madison Avenue
New York, NY 10016

John F. Saladino
Saladino Group, Inc.
200 Lexington Avenue, Suite 1600
New York, NY 10016

John Schneider
P.O. Box 1457
Pebble Beach, CA 93953

Teri Seidman Interiors
150 East 61st Street
New York, NY 10021

Carol Shawn Interiors
219 Baltimore Avenue
Corte Madera, CA 94925

Ho Sang Shin, Antine Associates
1028 Arcadian Way
Fort Lee, NJ 07024

Eduardo Souto de Moura
Souto Moura - Arquitectos, Lda.
Rua do Aleixo, 53
4150 Porto
Portugal

Spiegel Catalog
P.O. Box 182555
Columbus, OH 43218

Lenny Steinberg Design Associates
2517 Ocean Front Walk
Venice, CA

Charles Stewart Architecture
85 Liberty Ship Way, #111
Sausalito, CA 94965

Janice Sugita
J.S. and Associates
312 Tajon Place
Rancho Palos Verdes, CA 90274

Timothy Techler
Techler Design Group, Inc.
46 Waltham Street, Suite 301
Boston, MA 02118

Christopher Thompson
Talis, Inc.
2605 Western Avenue
Seattle, WA 98121

Duncan Todd
T 2
414 Mason Street, Suite 702
San Francisco, CA 95102

Robert Truax
360 Arguello Boulevard
San Francisco, CA 94118

Unique Hotels and Resorts
840 Apollo Street, Suite 314
El Segundo, CA 90245

Kelly Wearstler
KWID
113 Ω N. La Brea Avenue
Los Angeles, CA 90036

Jeffry Weisman
545 Sansome Street
San Francisco, CA 94111

Randall Whitehead
Randall Whitehead International
1246 28th Street
San Francisco, CA 94107

Kendel Wilkinson
550 15th Street
San Francisco, CA 94103

Dianna Wong
315 West 9th Street
Los Angeles, CA 90015

Your Space
161 Natoma Street
San Francisco, CA 94105

Alfredo Zaparolli
Techlinea Design Associates
2325 3rd Street, Suite 430
San Francisco, CA 94107

Russell Abraham
309 4th Street #108
Oakland, CA 94607

Luis Ferreira Alves
Rua de Alegria
Parque Habitacional do Lima
Entrada 29
Habitacao 3A Porto, Portugal

Dennis Anderson
48 Lucky Drive
Greenbrae, CA 94904

Jaime Ardiles-Arce
730 Fifth Avenue
New York, NY 10019

Bjorg Arnarsdottir
Twist Visuals, Inc.
517 Sixth Avenue
New York, NY 10011

Tony Berardi
Photofields
36W830 Stonebridge Lane
St. Charles, IL 60175

Brady Architectural Photography
1010 University Avenue, #823
San Diego, CA 92103

Christopher Covey
Christopher Covey Photography
1780 Vista Del Mar Dr.
Ventura, CA 93001
805-648-3067

Grey Crawford Photography
2924 Park Center Drive
Los Angeles, CA 90068

Jacques Dirand
10 Pessage Doisy
75017 Paris, France

Dennis Gilbert
Arcaid
The Factory
2 Acre Road
Kingston-pon-Thames
Surrey KT2 6EF England

David Glomb
71340 Estellita Drive
Rancho Mirage, CA 92270

Art Gray
171 Pier Avenue, #272
Santa Monica, CA 90405

Timothy Hursley
The Arkansas Office, Inc.
1911 West Markham
Little Rock, AR 72203

Warren Jagger Photography, Inc.
150 Chestnut Street, 7th Floor
Providence, RI 02903

Peter Jaquith
6 Pleasant Street
Beverly, MA 01915

Tim Lee Photography
2 Zachary Lane
New Milford, CT 06776

Chris A. Little
P.O. Box 467221
Atlanta, GA 30346

David Duncan Livingston
1036 Erica Road
Mill Valley, CA 94705
www.davidduncanlivingston.com

Peter Margonelli
20 Debrosses Street
New York, NY 10013-1704

John Martin Photography
68 Ashton Avenue
San Francisco, CA 94112

E. Andrew McKinney
McKinney Photography
180 1/2 10th Avenue
San Francisco, CA

Jeff McNamara
68 Vista
Easton, CT 06612

Colin McRae Photography
1061 Folsom Street
San Francisco, CA 94103

Matthew Millman Photography
821 Richmond Street
El Cerrito, CA 94530

Ira Nowinski Photographer
10 Allen Court
San Rafael, CA 94901

Eric Oxendorf Studio
1442 North Franklin Place
Milwaukee, WI 53202

Peter Paige Associates Inc.
269 Parkside Road
Harrington Park, NJ 07640

Eric Roth
Eric Roth Studio
337 Summer Street
Boston, MA 02210

Bill Rothschild
19 Judith Lane
Wesley Hills, NY 10952

Douglas Salin Photographer
647 Joost Avenue
San Francisco, CA 94127

David Story
5609 Corson Avenue S.
Seattle, WA 98108

Tim Street-Porter
2074 Watsonia Terrace
Los Angeles, CA 90068

John Sutton
8 Main Street
Pt. San Quentin, CA 94964

Steve Vierra Photography
P.O. Box 1827
Sandwich, MA 02563

Dominique Vorillon
1636 Silverwood Terrace
Los Angeles, CA 90026

William Waldron
Achard & Associates
611 Broadway, Suite 803
New York, NY 10012

Alan Weintraub Photography
1832A Mason Street
San Francisco, CA 94133

Eric Zepeda
4x5
1451 Stevenson Street, Studio A
San Francisco, CA 94103

Ann McArdle is a freelance writer who lives and works in Gloucester, Massachusetts. Recently retired from a career in publishing, she writes on a wide range of topics.

Her books on interior design include the series *Minimal Interiors, Romantic Interiors, Elegant Interiors, Natural Interiors,* and *Harmonious Interiors,* all published by Rockport Publishers. Her book, *Stephanie's Angels,* will be appearing in 2000, published by Twin Lights Publishers.

In her free time, McArdle studies yoga and tutors at Gloucester's Wellspring House, Inc. in their Foundations Program teaching career skills to women in transition.